BUDŌ
Teachings of the Founder of Aikidō

BUDŌ

Teachings of
the Founder of
Aikidō

Morihei Ueshiba

Introduction by
Kisshōmaru Ueshiba

KODANSHA INTERNATIONAL
Tokyo • New York • London

Distributed in the United States by Kodansha America, Inc., 575 Lexington Avenue, New York, New York 10022, and in the United Kingdom and continental Europe by Kodansha Europe, Ltd., 95 Aldwych, London WC2B 4JF. Published by Kodansha International, Ltd., 17-14 Otowa 1-chome, Bunkyo-ku, Tokyo 112-8652, and Kodansha America, Inc.

First edition, 1991
First paperback edition, 1996
01 02 03 04 05   10 9 8 7 6 5

LCC 90-25266
ISBN 4-7700-2070-8

www.thejapanpage.com

CONTENTS

PART I

INTRODUCTION
by Kisshōmaru Ueshiba

The Life of Morihei Ueshiba

Morihei Ueshiba was born on December 14, 1883, in Tanabe, Wakayama Prefecture. He was the fourth child and eldest son of Yoroku Ueshiba, a well-to-do farmer who owned two hectares (about five acres) of prime land. His father was a widely respected member of the local community who had served on the village council for twenty years, while his mother, Yuki Itokawa, came from a landowning family of noble descent.

Around the age of seven Morihei was sent to Jizōdera, a nearby Buddhist temple of the Shingon sect, to study the Confucian classics and Buddhist scriptures. He was enthralled by the miracle tales told of the Buddhist saint Kōbō Daishi, and he began to experience recurring dreams, a tendency that caused his father some concern. Yoroku therefore encouraged him in more physical pursuits, and taught him sumo and swimming.

Morihei graduated from Tanabe Higher Elementary School, and was admitted to the newly established Tanabe Prefectural Middle School at the age of thirteen. He left middle school before graduating, however, and went to the Yoshida Abacus Institute. Upon obtaining his diploma, he found employment at the Tanabe Tax Office, where his duties included the assessment of land values.

Morihei resigned from the tax office in 1902, after joining a popular movement against new fishing legislation, and went to Tokyo with the aim of making a fresh start as a businessman. For a time he worked as a live-in employee in the commercial district of Nihombashi, before setting up his own stationery and school supplies company, Ueshiba Trading. More importantly, it was during this first stay in Tokyo that Morihei began his study of the martial arts, learning traditional *jūjutsu* and *kenjutsu*. Later in the same year, however, he developed beri-beri and was forced to leave Tokyo. Soon after his return to Tanabe, he married Hatsu Itokawa (born 1881), whom he had known since childhood.

In 1903 Morihei enlisted in the 37th regiment of the Fourth Division in Osaka, where he was nicknamed "the King of Soldiers" for his skill with the bayonet and his hardworking, honest character. When the Russo-Japanese War broke out in the following year, he was sent to the front as a corporal, and returned having been promoted to the rank of sergeant for outstanding bravery in the field. During periods of leisure from military life Morihei continued to pursue his interest in the martial arts, attending Masakatsu Nakai's *dōjō* in Sakai, where he learned the Gotō school of Yagyū-*ryū jūjutsu*.

In 1907 Morihei was discharged from the army and returned to Tanabe, where he worked on the family farm and participated in village politics, becoming the leader of the local Young Men's Association.

During this period his father engaged the *judōka* Kiyoichi Takagi, who was then visiting Tanabe, to act as Morihei's teacher, and converted the family barn into a *dōjō*. It was here that Morihei learned the Kōdōkan style of *judō*. He also continued to attend the Nakai Dōjō and received a certificate from the Gotō school.

Morihei remained in Tanabe for the next three years, involving himself in many local activities. In 1910 (the year that his eldest daughter, Matsuko, was born) Morihei became interested in a government plan to settle the northern island of Hokkaido. He decided to form a settlement group and appealed for volunteers from the local Young Men's Association. He became the leader of the Kishū group, consisting of fifty-four households (over eighty people), and in March 1912 they left Tanabe for Hokkaido. They arrived in May, and settled at Shirataki, near the village of Yobetsu, a site chosen by Morihei on an earlier trip.

This area, where the present-day village of Shirataki still stands, was then a wasteland, and the colonists had to struggle against appalling weather and poor soil conditions to bring it under cultivation. Nevertheless, the Kishū group did eventually succeed in initiating a number of enterprises, including the cultivation of mint, horse rearing, and dairy farming, as well as establishing the beginnings of a timber industry. Morihei did his utmost to ensure the success of the venture, and initiated several projects, including the construction of a shopping street in Shirataki, the improvement of housing conditions, and the founding of a primary school. It was during his Hokkaido period that Morihei, while staying at an inn in Engaru, made the acquaintance of Sōkaku Takeda, the well-known master of Daitō-*ryū*. He subsequently trained intensely with Takeda, and gained a certificate in Daitō-*ryū jūjutsu*.

Owing to the expansion of the timber industry, Shirataki was fast becoming a boom town. But on May 23, 1917, the village was completely destroyed by a disastrous fire. The following spring found Morihei, who had been elected a member of the village council, totally immersed in the reconstruction of Shirataki. In July that same year Morihei's eldest son, Takemori, was born.

In mid-November 1919 Morihei was shocked to receive the news that his father was seriously ill. He left Hokkaido to return to Tanabe, bringing his Shirataki period to a close after eight years.

On his return trip Morihei heard that the leader of the flourishing new religion Ōmoto-kyō, Ōnisaburō Deguchi, who was famous for his *chinkon kishin* (calming the spirit and returning to the divine) meditation techniques, was living in nearby Ayabe. Morihei decided to visit him, and remained in Ayabe until December 28. He asked Ōnisaburō to pray for his father, but Ōnisaburō replied, "Your father is all right as he is." These words made a deep impression on Morihei.

Yoroku Ueshiba died on January 2, 1920, aged 76. His death was a great blow to Morihei, and, after a period of emotional instability, he decided to move to Ayabe in search of a more spiritual life, under the guidance of Ōnisaburō Deguchi. He obtained a house behind the primary school within the sacred precincts of the Ōmoto-kyō, and it was there that he lived for the next eight years, until he moved to Tokyo in 1928.

During this period he enjoyed Ōnisaburō's absolute confidence, and took part in various spiritual practices of the sect. Also with Ōnisaburō's encouragement, Morihei converted part of his house into an eighteen-mat *dōjō*, and opened the Ueshiba Academy, where he taught introductory courses in the martial arts, mainly to Ōmoto-kyō followers. Sadly, Morihei's first year in Ayabe was marked by further personal tragedy: he lost both his sons through illness; Takemori died in August, aged three, and in September his second son, Kuniharu, died, aged one.

Morihei, at age thirty-eight, in front of his first *dōjō*. In 1920 Morihei and his family moved to the Ōmoto-kyō headquarters in Ayabe (near Kyoto). There the Ueshiba Academy was established, with Morihei teaching Daitō-*ryū aiki-jūjutsu* to Ōmoto-kyō followers.

Morihei (center) working in the Ōmoto-kyō headquarters' organic garden. Throughout his life, Morihei was passionately fond of farming. He believed that there was a special affinity between *budō* and agriculture, two activities that nourished life and promoted clean living and high thoughts.

In the year following Morihei's move to Ayabe, the instruction offered at the Ueshiba Academy gradually increased in range and depth, and word began to spread that there was an exceptional master of the martial arts living in Ayabe. The number of non-Ōmoto-kyō followers enrolling at the Ueshiba Academy began to increase, and many sailors from the nearby naval base at Maizuru came to train there.

On February 11, 1921, the authorities suddenly clamped down on the sect in what later became known as the First Ōmoto Incident, and several people, including Ōnisaburō, were arrested. Fortunately the incident had no effect on the Ueshiba Academy. Nineteen twenty-one was also the year of my birth.

Over the next two years Morihei tried to help Ōnisaburō, who had been released on bail, to rebuild the Ōmoto-kyō. He took over administration of about nine hundred *tsubo* of Tennōdaira land, which he farmed while he continued to teach at the Ueshiba Academy. In this way he was able to realize in his everyday life the belief that there is an essential unity between the martial arts and agriculture, something that was close to his heart and was to be a recurring theme throughout his life.

From around this period Morihei's practice of the martial arts gradually began to take on a spiritual character, as he became more and more absorbed by the study of *kotodama*. This led him little by little to break away from the conventions of Yagyū-*ryū* and Daitō-*ryū jūjutsu*, and to develop his own original approach, using applied principles and technique together, to break down the barriers between mind, spirit, and body. In 1922 this approach was formally named *"aiki-bujutsu,"* but it became known to the general public as Ueshiba-*ryū aiki-bujutsu.*

In 1924 Morihei embarked on an adventure that was to prove crucial to his spiritual development. On February 13 he secretly left Ayabe with Ōnisaburō, bound for Manchuria and Mongolia, in search of a holy land where they could establish a new world government based on religious precepts. On the 15th, they arrived in Mukden, where they met with Lu Chang K'uei, a famous Manchurian warlord. Together with Lu, they led the Northwest Autonomous Army (also known as the Mongolian Independence Army) into the interior of the country. At this time Morihei was given the Chinese name Wang Shou Kao. However, their expedition was ill-fated; they were victims of a plot concocted by another warlord, Chang Tso Lin, and when they reached Baian Dalai on June 20, they found the Chinese troops waiting to arrest them. Morihei, Ōnisaburō, and four others were sentenced to death. Fortunately, just before they were due to be executed, a member of the Japanese consular staff intervened and secured their release and safe return to Japan.

Morihei tried to resume his former life, uniting the practice of the martial arts and farming by teaching at the Ueshiba Academy and working on the Tennōdaira farm. He also became interested in *sōjutsu* (spear technique), and continued his intensive practice of swordsmanship and *jūjutsu.* Things were not the same, however. He had been deeply affected by the expedition to Manchuria and

In 1924 Morihei accompanied Ōnisaburō Deguchi on the Great Mongolian Adventure. Hoping to create a "heaven on earth" in Mongolia, Ōnisaburō and his group made it to the border of that remote land only to be arrested by a Chinese warlord and threatened with execution. This photograph shows the group in leg irons prior to their release into the custody of the local Japanese consul. Morihei, third from left and standing next to Ōnisaburō, is apparently also bound by the arms.

The founder on a pilgrimage to the sacred Nachi Falls in Kumano. Morihei was deeply affected by his many encounters with death during the Great Mongolian Adventure, and upon his return to Japan he intensified his search for the true meaning of *budō*. He frequently secluded himself in the mountains to engage in ascetic discipline, as shown in this photo, and at age forty-two Morihei underwent a profound enlightenment experience that made him invincible as a martial artist.

Morihei and Ōnisaburō surrounded by a group of Ōmoto-kyō followers. Extremely gifted and wildly eccentric, Morihei and Ōnisaburō were two of the greatest visionaries of all time.

Mongolia, in particular by his experiences of facing death under gunfire, and he had found that he could see flashes of light indicating the path of oncoming bullets. The discovery of this intuitive sense was a profound experience for Morihei, and after returning to Japan, he frequently encountered situations where he felt manifestations of a spiritual force.

In the spring of 1925 Morihei met a naval officer and master of *kendō*. He accepted the officer's challenge and defeated him without actually fighting, because he could sense the direction in which the blows would fall before the officer's wooden sword could strike him. Immediately after this encounter he went to wash at a well, where he experienced a complete serenity of body and spirit. He suddenly felt that he was bathing in a golden light that poured down from heaven. It was a unique experience for him, a revelation, and he felt reborn, as though his body and spirit had been turned into gold. At the same time the unity of the universe and the self became clear to him and he came to understand one by one the other philosophical principles on which aikidō is based. It was also in this way that he realized that it would be better to name his creation *aiki-budō*, rather than *aiki-bujutsu*. (The substitution of the character *dō* in the place of *jutsu* changes the meaning from the martial art of *aiki* to the martial way of *aiki*.)

As *aiki-budō* became better known, it attracted a number of distinguished followers, including Admiral Isamu Takeshita. In the fall of 1925 Morihei was invited to visit the admiral in Tokyo. He stayed at the residence of former Prime Minister Gombei Yamamoto, where he gave a martial arts display in front of a number of dignitaries, all of whom were greatly impressed. Morihei also spent twenty-one days teaching the martial arts at the Crown Prince's Palace.

In the spring of 1926 he again went to Tokyo at Admiral Takeshita's invitation. He taught at the Imperial Court and Imperial Household Ministry, as well as teaching army and navy personnel and people connected with the world of finance. Morihei's stay in Tokyo became somewhat prolonged, but in the summer he fell ill with an intestinal disorder and was forced to return to Ayabe to rest.

In February 1927, having received an invitation from Admiral Takeshita, Morihei felt he had no alternative but to leave Ayabe for the third time. With Ōnisaburō's blessing, he decided to make the move a permanent one and to devote his energies solely to establishing himself in Tokyo as a teacher of the martial arts.

After two years in temporary accommodations, Morihei moved to a house near Sengaku temple in Kuruma-chō, where he converted two eight-mat rooms into a *dōjō*. His students included Isamu Fujita, Shōyō Matsui, and Kaizan Nakazato, and Kabuki actor Kikugorō Ennosuke VI.

In 1930 Morihei obtained a villa in Ushigome, Wakamatsu-chō, and began the construction of a new *dōjō*. While the work was in progress he set up a temporary *dōjō* in Mejirodai, and it was there that he received a visit from Jigorō Kanō, the founder of *judō* and head of the Kōdōkan, in October 1930. Kanō was most impressed by Morihei's technique and praised him highly, saying, "This is my ideal *budō*." Kanō subsequently sent two of his students, Jirō

Takeda and Minoru Mochizuki, to train under Morihei.

Another memorable visit in 1930 was that of Major-General Makoto Miura. He was skeptical about the new *budō*, and visited the *dōjō* only in order to defeat Morihei. The founder overcame Miura's doubts so completely, however, that he enrolled as a student on the spot. Subsequently, at the request of the same major-general, Morihei became an instructor at the Toyama Military Academy.

In April 1931 a full-scale eighty-mat *aiki-budō dōjō*, inaugurated as the Kōbukan, was completed in Wakamatsu-chō, at the same site where the main *dōjō* stands today. Many students enrolled, including Hisao Kamata, Hajime Iwata, Kaoru Funabashi, Tsutomu Yūgawa, and Rinjirō Shirata, and for the next ten years *aiki-budō* experienced its first golden age. At the same time the Kōbukan was popularly known as the "hell *dōjō*," because of the extraordinarily intense training practiced there.

The next few years were extremely busy ones for Morihei, as he was teaching not only at the Kōbukan, but also at many other *dōjō* that had started up in Tokyo and Osaka. The main *dōjō* were the Ōtsuka Dōjō in Koishikawa (sponsored by Seiji Noma, the chairman of Kodansha) and the Fujimi-chō Dōjō in Iidabashi, and in Osaka the Sonezaki Dōjō, the Suida Dōjō, and the Chausuyama Dōjō. Notable *uchi-deshi* (live-in students) at this time were Shigemi Yonekawa, Zenzaburō Akazawa, Gōzō Shioda, and Tetsumi Hoshi.

Morihei also taught at police stations in the Osaka area on the

Morihei with the initial group of live-in disciples of the Kōbukan. The Kōbukan, opened in 1931 in Tokyo, attracted talented young trainees from all over the country. Although not shown here, there were also several outstanding female students in the early days of the Kōbukan.

recommendation of one of his followers, Kenji Tomita, chief of Osaka prefectural police and later governor of Nagano Prefecture and chief cabinet secretary. In addition, he was becoming more involved in teaching at the Asahi Newspaper in Osaka, and through the Japan Industrial Club he had many opportunities to teach people from the financial world.

In 1932 the Society for the Promotion of Japanese Martial Arts was founded, and in 1933 Morihei became its president. In May 1933 a full-time training hall, called the Takeda Dōjō, was set up in Hyogo Prefecture. Dozens of students came to live there, putting into practice the founder's ideal of uniting the martial arts and agriculture.

By the mid-thirties Morihei had become famous throughout the martial arts world. Even more than for his mastery of the various traditional Japanese martial arts, he came to public attention for the epoch-making nature of his own original creation, "the union of spirit, mind, and body" in *aiki*, formally called *aiki-budō*. During this period Morihei was practicing *kendō* very intensively at the Kōbukan Dōjō, and a number of *kendō* practitioners frequented the *dōjō*, including Kiyoshi Nakakura, who became Morihei's son-in-law in 1932.

In September 1939 Morihei was invited to Manchuria to attend a public exhibition of the martial arts. There he fought the ex-sumo wrestler Tenryū and pinned him with one finger. Morihei continued his visits to Manchuria even after the outbreak of the Pacific War, taking up advisory posts at various institutions, including Kenkoku

Morihei in his early fifties. By this time, Morihei was renowned throughout the country as Japan's top martial artist.

Morihei with Kiyoshi Nakakura, circa 1933. Naka-kura, who was briefly Morihei's son-in-law, was primarily a swordsman. After leaving the Kōbukan, Nakakura went on to become the top *kendō* man in modern Japan. Now near eighty, Nakakura remains active as a competitor.

Morihei in 1940, at age fifty-seven, photographed during a visit to Manchuria.

University, with which he became particularly involved. His last visit to Manchuria was in 1942, when he attended the celebrations for the tenth anniversary of the founding of the Japanese-sponsored state of Manchukuo at the invitation of the Greater Martial Arts Association, and gave a demonstration of the martial arts in the presence of Emperor Pu'Yi.

On April 30, 1940, the Kōbukan was granted the status of an incorporated foundation by the Ministry of Health and Welfare. The first president of the foundation was Admiral Isamu Takeshita. In the same year the police academy where Morihei was teaching adopted *aiki-budō* as an official curriculum subject.

With the outbreak of the Pacific War, one after another, the students at the Tokyo *dōjō* went to the front. I was then a student at Waseda University High School, and together with Kisaburō Ōzawa and other young aikidō students, I was given the responsibility of maintaining the *dōjō*.

Also in 1941 *aiki-budō* was assimilated into the Butokukai (a governmental body uniting all the martial arts under one organization). Morihei appointed Minoru Hirai to represent and manage the Kōbukan in the Aiki Section of the Butokukai. It was around this time that the name aikidō first came into use.

In reaction to the makeshift nature of the new arrangements, made in a time of emergency, whereby aikidō was reduced to a section of the Butokukai, and in order to preserve the spirit of the *budō* he had created for future generations, Morihei reestablished the base of the aikidō organization in Ibaragi Prefecture. Leaving me in charge of the *dōjō* in Wakamatsu-chō, Morihei moved to Iwama with his wife, living there frugally in a converted barn until after the end of the war.

In Iwama, Morihei began the construction of what he called the *ubuya* (birthing room), or inner sanctum, of aikidō: a complex including the Aiki Shrine and an outdoor *dōjō*. The inner building of the Aiki Shrine, which features exquisite carvings, was completed in 1944; the Aiki Dōjō, now known as the Ibaragi Dōjō Annex of the Aiki Shrine, was completed in 1945, just before the end of the war.

Forty-three deities are enshrined at the Aiki Shrine as guardian deities of aikidō. Morihei himself planned the shrine precincts, following the principles of *kotodama*. For example, the main building, the prayer hall, the *torii*, and the layout as a whole follow the law

In the early stages of World War II, Morihei's counsel was sought by military leaders and prime ministers, but soon the carnage made him emotionally and physically ill. In 1942 Morihei abruptly resigned all of his official positions and retired with his wife to a little hut in the woods of Iwama in Ibaragi Prefecture (left). There Morihei farmed and arranged for the construction of the Aiki Shrine (right). In 1942 during the darkest period of human history, Morihei was moved to call his system aikidō, "The Way of Harmony and Love."

of the three universal principles, that is, the triangle, the circle, and the square, symbolic of breathing exercises in *kotodama* study. "When the triangle, the circle, and the square are united in spherical rotation, a state of perfect clarity results. This is the basis of aikidō," Morihei explained.

Throughout the war, I struggled to preserve the Kōbukan Dōjō, despite the worsening situation and the massive bombing of Tokyo by the U.S. Air Force. The *dōjō* escaped damage, but after the war it was used as a shelter by over thirty homeless families, so practice could no longer continue there. The headquarters of aikidō was therefore moved to Iwama, where Morihei continued to live quietly, farming and teaching young people from the surrounding area.

After the war the martial arts went into decline for a time, and the future of aikidō, too, was in doubt. However, Morihei had faith in the new aikidō, and together we worked hard to establish its place in postwar Japan. When it seemed that the confusion prevailing in the immediate aftermath of the war had abated somewhat, it was decided to move the headquarters of aikidō back to Tokyo. On February 9, 1948, the Ministry of Education granted permission to reestablish the Aikikai, with a revised charter. During that time the main *dōjō* in Tokyo was renamed the Ueshiba Dōjō and World Headquarters of Aikidō.

After the establishment of the Aikikai, I was given the responsi-

Morihei praying for world peace during a ceremony marking the beginning of the new year. Morihei was often described as being the most religious person in Japan. In his later years, Morihei spent much of his time in study, prayer, and meditation.

Morihei, aged sixty-eight, posing (left) for a stylized portrait depicting him as a Shintō deity (right). Morihei is portrayed as a muscular Shintō guardian spirit possessing the three sacred treasures: the pacifying sword, the mirror of illumination, and the jewel of perfection (his round belly).

bility of consolidating the existing organization and planning its future development. Meanwhile, Morihei remained in Iwama, absorbed in contemplation and martial arts practice.

From 1950 onward Morihei once more began to travel around Japan in response to invitations to teach, lecture, and give demonstrations. As he reached the age of seventy, Morihei's superb technique flowed increasingly from his vastness of spirit, in contrast to the fierceness and physical strength that had characterized his earlier years. He came to place greater emphasis on the loving nature of aikidō. (The first character of aikidō, "*ai*," which means harmony, is read in the same way as the character meaning love. In his later years, Morihei stressed the equivalence of these two meanings.)

In 1954 the headquarters of aikidō was moved to Tokyo, and the Tokyo *dōjō* took the official title of the Aikikai Foundation: the Hombu Dōjō of Aikidō. In September 1956 the Aikikai held the first public demonstration of martial arts since the end of the war on the rooftop of the Takashimaya department store in Nihombashi, Tokyo. The demonstration lasted five days, and made a deep impression on the foreign dignitaries present. Morihei had been adamantly opposed to giving such public demonstrations, but he understood that Japan had entered a new era, and consented in order to further the development of aikidō.

As aikidō became established in the popular consciousness, the number of students from all over the world rapidly increased. In Japan itself, new *dōjō* were set up all over the country, and aikidō spread into universities, government offices, and companies, heralding its second golden age.

As Morihei became older, he took a less active role in the management of the Aikikai, leaving me in charge of the instruction at the Hombu Dōjō. However, he continued to give demonstrations, and in January 1960 NTV broadcasted "The Master of Aikidō," a program that captured the founder's techniques on film.

On May 14, 1960, an aikidō demonstration was sponsored by the Aikikai in Shinjuku, Tokyo. On that occasion Morihei made a deep impression on his audience with a demonstration entitled "The Essence of Aikidō."

Later that year Morihei, together with Yosaburō Uno, a *kyūdō* tenth *dan*, was given the *Shijuhōshō* Award by Emperor Hirohito. Only three people from the martial arts world had ever been given this award before: the *judō* master Kyūzō Mifune, and the kendō masters Kinnosuke Ogawa and Seiji Mochida.

On February 28, 1961, Morihei went to the United States on the invitation of the Hawaii Aikikai. During this visit the founder made the following statement:

I have come to Hawaii in order to build a "silver bridge." Until now, I have remained in Japan, building a "golden

The seventy-year-old Morihei training in a waterfall with his son, Kisshōmaru. Throughout his career, Morihei was constantly refining and expanding his art. "This old man must still train and train," he said shortly before his death.

Here Morihei executes a throw: "Aikidō is
the principle of nonresistance."

bridge" to unite Japan, but henceforward, I wish to build a
bridge to bring the different countries of the world together
through the harmony and love contained in aikidō. I think
that *aiki*, offspring of the martial arts, can unite the people of
the world in harmony, in the true spirit of *budō*, enveloping
the world in unchanging love.

On August 7, 1962, a great festival was held at the Aiki Shrine in
Iwama to celebrate Morihei's sixtieth anniversary as a practitioner
of the martial arts, and in 1964 he received a special award from
Emperor Hirohito in recognition of his contributions to the martial
arts.

The groundbreaking ceremony for the construction of a new
Hombu Dōjō in Tokyo was held on March 14, 1967. On the same
day, Morihei performed the first ceremonial plowing of the new
year in Iwama. On December 15 that year the new *dōjō*, a modern
three-story building made of reinforced concrete, was completed.
One of the rooms was used by the founder as a study and bedroom,
and this room is now known as the Founder's Materials Room.

On January 12, 1968, a commemorative ceremony was held in
honor of the completion of the new Hombu Dōjō, and Morihei
spoke about the essence of aikidō technique. Later that year Morihei
was to give what was to be his last demonstration of aikidō, at the
Kōkaidō in Hibiya, in honor of the completion of the new building.

On January 15, 1969, Morihei attended the New Year's celebrations in the Hombu Dōjō. Although he appeared to be in good
health, his physical condition rapidly deteriorated, and he passed
away peacefully on April 26, 1969, at 5 P.M. A vigil was held at the
Hombu Dōjō on May 1, starting at 7:10 P.M. , and on the same day

the founder was given a posthumous award by Emperor Hirohito. His ashes were buried in the cemetery of the Ueshiba family temple in Tanabe, and strands of the founder's hair were enshrined at the Aiki Shrine in Iwama, the Ueshiba family cemetery in Ayabe, and at the Kumano Grand Shrine.

Kisshōmaru Ueshiba was elected to succeed his father as Aiki Dōshu *by a unanimous decision of the Aikikai, on June 14, 1970.*

Translated by Louella Matsunaga

Morihei demonstrating *tai-no-henka*, transforming the body according to the circumstance, in dynamic fashion. Morihei's piercing *kiai* could be heard half a mile away.

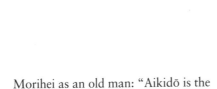

Morihei as an old man: "Aikidō is the manifestation of love."

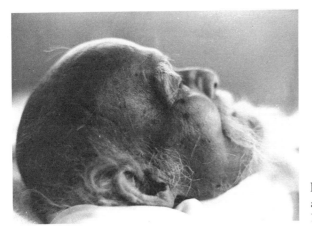

Death portrait of Morihei. The founder of aikidō returned to the Source on April 26, 1969, aged eighty-six.

Morihei with the sword of *aiki* which "empowers one to cut through and destroy all evil, and to pacify the world."

PART II

BUDŌ
by Morihei Ueshiba

Translator's Foreword

Budō *was published and privately circulated in 1938 when Morihei was fifty-five years old, his physical and mental prime. This is the only instruction manual for which Morihei himself actually posed for the photographs illustrating the techniques, and it contains one of the few comprehensive explanations of his philosophy.*

Despite having been put together over fifty years ago in a very different era, Budō—like all true classics—has a timeless quality to it. Other than a few stock references to the old imperial order and some archaic language, the text is hardly dated at all. Morihei's message that budō *is a spiritual path leading to enlightenment, peace, harmony, truth, goodness, and beauty remained constant over the years. The formulation of the mature system of aikidō in 1942 was based on the principles and techniques enunciated in* Budō.

The text itself is terse and cryptic, as is the custom with such manuals. It also assumes that the teachings it presents will be augmented by oral explanations from qualified instructors. The translation is as literal as possible and follows the original organization of the book, which was somewhat haphazard.

Three illustrations which were misplaced have been put in the proper order, and mistakes in labeling the illustrations have also been corrected.

John Stevens

TEACHINGS OF THE PATH

Budō[1] is a divine path established by the gods that leads to truth, goodness, and beauty; it is a spiritual path reflecting the unlimited, absolute nature of the universe and the ultimate grand design of creation.

Through the virtue acquired from devoted practice, one can perceive the principles of heaven and earth. Such techniques originate from the subtle interaction of water and fire,[2] revealing the path of heaven and earth and the spirit of the imperial way; these applied techniques also display the marvelous functioning of *kotodama*,[3] the principle that directs and harmonizes all things in the world, resulting in the unification of heaven, earth, god, and humankind. Such virtue generates light and heat, forming the divine sword of spiritual harmonization between heaven, earth, and humankind; when the situation arises, armed with that sword of harmonization and acting according to the principles of heaven and earth, one can continuously slash through falsehood and evil, clearing a path leading toward a beautiful and pristine world. Thus totally awakened, one can freely utilize all elements contained in heaven and earth throughout spring, summer, autumn, and winter. Reform your perception of how the universe actually looks and acts; change the martial techniques into a vehicle of purity, goodness, and beauty; and master these things. When the sword of harmonization linking heaven, earth, and humankind is manifest, one is liberated, able to purify and forge the self.

METHODS

You yourself and all that you possess should be dedicated to majestic causes; as warriors on the martial path, it is our duty to follow the will of the gods, externally and internally, and serve the people. In *budō*, we guide the enemy where we please. The true purpose of the methods described herein is to teach a warrior how to receive and fill his mind and body with a valorous spirit—one must polish one's *ki*[4] and forge the spirit within the realm of life and death. Practice these methods intently with your entire mind and body, temper yourself ceaselessly, and advance on and on; weld yourself to heaven and earth and unify practice and enlightenment. Realize that your mind and body must be permeated with the soul of a warrior, enlightened wisdom, and deep calm.

POEMS OF THE PATH [5]

Rely on the majesty
of the lord
who rules
our world
and advance bravely.

O gods of heaven and earth!
We beseech you to guide us
toward the precious techniques of *ki*
that calm the soul
and purify all things.

"*Ei!!*"
Cut down the enemy
lurking inside oneself
and guide all things with
shouts of "*Yaa!*" and "*Iei!*" [6]

True *budō*
cannot be described
by words or letters;
the gods will not allow you
to make such explanations.

Techniques of the Sword [7]
cannot be encompassed
by words or letters.
Do not rely on such things—
move on toward enlightenment!

Deep and mysterious
the grand design
of the Path of the Sword—
place its heat and light
in your heart.

Foster and polish
the warrior spirit
while serving in the world;
illuminate the Path
in accordance with the divine will. [8]

Taught to us by the gods,
the grand design of the Path
follows the divine.
The Path of *aiki* [9]
revealed by the Angel of Purification. [10]

Forge the spirit
according to the divine will;
seek the light and heat
of the Universal Sword
and move on toward enlightenment.

Let our forging
bear fruit as
the body of *aiki*.
Whom are we to thank?
Our imperial leader.

The will of the gods
permeating body and soul
is *aiki*—polish that sword
and make its brilliance
known throughout this world.

Ceaselessly polish
the Sacred Sword
and bring forth its divinity;
a holy warrior
serves the gods.

Forge the spirit
according to the divine will;
the Divine Sword should shine
clear and bright,
manifesting the grace of the gods.

The penetrating brilliance of a sword
wielded by a follower of the Way
strikes at the evil enemy
lurking deep within
one's own body and soul.

Crystal clear,
sharp and bright,
the Sacred Sword
allows no opening for
evil to roost.

Not a weakness anywhere—
brighten up the world
and make the Path of the Sword
manifest in the bodies and souls
of all people.

The Path of the Sword,
unlimited and unfathomable,
should be opened to the world
and made manifest in the
bodies and souls of all people.

Warriors!
Rally around and brandish the
Universal Sword.
Shine brightly and
reveal it to the world.

Keep this in your heart:
sword techniques are not things.
Follow the divine—
the soul does not speak
yet its divinity shines.

No voice can be heard,
no heart can be seen;
follow the divine
and there will be nothing
to ask of the gods.

"Sincerity"[11]
is said to be shown by those
following the Path of the Sword;
you may petition the gods for it
but there is no need for them to reply.

No voice to see,
no heart to hear—
sword techniques.
Initially the world
learns directly from the gods

Steadfast and sure,
giving life to the cosmos—
the Sacred Sword.
Deep learning and *budō* are the
two blades of the gods' grand design.

From ancient times
deep learning and *budō* have been
the two wheels of the Path;
through the virtue of practice
enlighten both body and soul.

At the instant
a warrior faces
an enemy
all things serve
to make the teachings more focused.

When learning
becomes superficial,
follow the guidance
of the sword
in both body and soul.

THE ESSENCE OF TECHNIQUE

1. THE PRINCIPLE OF ADJUSTING MIND AND BODY

The appearance of an "enemy" should be thought of as an opportunity to test the sincerity of one's mental and physical training, to see if one is actually responding according to the divine will. When facing the realm of life and death in the form of an enemy's sword, one must be firmly settled in mind and body, and not at all intimidated; without providing your opponent the slightest opening, control his mind in a flash and move where you will—straight, diagonally, or in any other appropriate direction. Enter deeply, mentally as well as physically, transform your entire body into a true sword, and vanquish your foe. This is *yamato-damashii*,[12] the principle behind the divine sword that manifests the soul of our nation.

In essence, the sword is the soul of a warrior and a manifestation of the true nature of the universe; thus, when you draw a sword you are holding your soul in your hands. Know that when two warriors face each other with swords, the body and soul of each individual is illuminated as they come together in a world that needs to be rid of falsehood and evil. [An enemy that appears along] the Great Path of divinely inspired swordsmanship enables a warrior to activate universal principles, and thus serves as an aid to the harmonization of all elements of heaven and earth, body and soul—glories that endure forever.

Our enlightened ancestors developed true *budō* based on humanity, love, and sincerity; its heart consists of sincere bravery, sincere wisdom, sincere love, and sincere empathy. These four spiritual virtues should be incorporated in the single sword of diligent training; constantly forge the spirit and body and let the brilliance of the transforming sword permeate your entire being.

Sports are widely practiced nowadays, and they are good for physical exercise. Warriors, too, train the body, but they also use the body as a vehicle to train the mind, calm the spirit, and find goodness and beauty, dimensions that sports lack. Training in *budō* fosters valor, sincerity, fidelity, goodness, and beauty, as well as making the body strong and healthy.

The Path is exceedingly vast. From ancient times to the present, even the greatest sages were unable to perceive and comprehend the entire truth; the explanations and teachings of masters and saints only express part of the whole. It is not possible for anyone to speak of such things in their entirety—just head for the light and heat, learn from the gods, and through the virtue of devoted practice become one with the divine. Seek enlightenment along this edge.

2. TRAINING METHODS

The best strategy relies upon unlimited responses. Pursue the Glorious Path, use the one to strike the many, and then the one will open the way to ten thousand vital principles; forge ten thousand swords, take charge, and attain the ultimate. Always keep the mind as bright and clear as the vast sky, the great ocean, and the highest mountain, empty of all thoughts.

Irimi [13]

If you are standing with your left foot forward when your opponent's sword strikes, rely on the principle of *kokyū*[14] timing to enter smoothly to his side; be prepared to strike a second opponent to the rear with your right hand. In an instant, advance deeply to his back with your left foot, keeping your right foot solidly based, and simultaneously cut down with your left hand to his rear. Step in with your right foot behind him without breaking your posture and down him with both hands. When your right foot is forward the procedure is reversed, and you must enter to your opponent's left.

Tai-no-henka[15] to the left and right

When it is necessary to adjust your movements, enter to the side in the manner described above, and then pivot on the front foot as quickly as a flash of lightning. (When your left foot is forward) swing around with the back leg and turn around to the right. Step out to the left and down any opponents who may be attacking from the front, back, left, or right. Whichever direction you move in, do not break your posture as you turn. The movement should involve a natural revolution of 360 degrees around a stable center.

Irimi-tenkan [16]

Face your opponent and enter as described above; once you have entered behind your opponent apply the principle of flexible movement, pivot on your front foot, turning freely in the appropriate direction, and down the surrounding opponents.

The imperial way involves constant battles. Train to summon up a powerful current of valorous *ki* and practice moving like a beam of light. Regarding technique, from ancient times it has been said that movements must fly like lightning and attacks must strike like thunder. Those principles can be seen with the eyes, but you must train diligently, seeking the divine, and master those principles that cannot be seen with human eyes—the functions of water and fire throughout the universe.

3. SHŌMEN TRAINING [17]

Striking with the right or left hand

Use of the *te-gatana* [hand-sword] (or fist): in order to deliver a devastating blow to an enemy, one must be enlightened to the principles of heaven and earth; one's mind and body must be linked to the divine, and there must be a perfect balance between the manifest and hidden, water and fire. Heaven, earth, and man must blend together as a single unified force—in this case a *te-gatana*—and one must move in harmony with the cosmos propelled by the divine; heat and light should radiate from your entire body. Without offering your opponent the slightest opening or allowing a break in the flow of *kokyū* and *ki,* you must be enlightened to the essence of "striking." Conversely, when the enemy strikes, always remain positive, calm, settled, and full of power, centered in the great spirit of the universe, and attuned to the will of the gods. Like this, even when you are surrounded by a host of enemies or other obstacles, you can anticipate any attack and shift direction to the left or right to escape.

Also, you must learn how to enter your opponent's mind and guide him along the path heaven and earth have indicated to you. For example, when surrounded by enemies, you will be able to draw them out to attack in the direction you want, turn in the appropriate manner, and then down them from behind. One must illuminate the border between life and death. Regardless of what may arise, one should be prepared to receive ninety-nine percent of an enemy's attack and stare death in the face in order to illuminate the path. Strike like thunder and fly more quickly than lightning—that is the way you should act. Keep these things in mind as you train and discern how to avoid entirely the pressure of an enemy's attack.

From ancient times, strategy was something taught as a natural expression of the august presence. Combat followed the dictates of heaven and earth, and one trained to react to contrasts in the flow of *kokyū*. In the training presented here, one must assume a certain distance. This must be done in accordance to the universal principles of the manifest and hidden, water and fire. One must learn to gauge, both physically and spiritually, the distance between self and other while remaining centered. Stand in conjunction with the universe, train to harness and unify the marvelous powers of water and fire—the true strategy of a real warrior has no limits. Open the realm of truth, purify and unite all the people of the world, and manifest the glory of the imperial will everywhere. Training in *budō* builds a true spiritual path leading to enlightened action. Furthermore, those sincerely training in other forms of *budō* manifest teachings that reflect the grand design of heaven and earth and lead to enlightenment. Hence, the virtues of bravery, wisdom, love, and empathy are united in the body and mind, creating a beautiful, valiant sword that directs us to greater and greater realizations. The law of the Great Path is established, the earth is protected, and each person becomes part of the process. This is how the warriors of Japan train; it is the act of opening the stone door.[18] If you learn to control the universal elements within the human heart, you can respond according to the principles of water and fire, yin and yang, when an enemy attacks. If he comes with *ki*, strike with *ki*; if he comes with water, strike with water; if he comes with fire, strike with fire. Think about such things and their relationship to modern scientific warfare when you train.

4. Yokomen Training

This is a blow delivered to the side of your opponent's head or down diagonally across his shoulder with your *te-gatana*. As soon as you sense a *yokomen* attack coming, draw it out; pull out slightly on your left foot, neutralize the blow by seizing the initiative and applying yin and yang (water and fire). Grasp your opponent's right wrist with your left hand, then add your right hand, take a big step in with your left foot, turn to the right, apply the principles of yin and yang, and throw him to the front. The precise use of the opponent's strength to your advantage depends upon perfect timing and a keen sense of the marvelous principle of the manifest and hidden qualities of water and fire; it can be applied directly or obliquely to down opponents attacking from either the left side or right side, and should be studied as an essential part of strategy. Such strategy is reinforced on the mats during the *yokomen* movements of daily practice.

Regarding technique, it is necessary to develop a strategy that utilizes all the physical conditions and elements that are directly at hand. The cosmic sword has many applications that can be only imparted orally and demonstrated in actual practice.

5. HAND TECHNIQUES

The hands, feet, and hips must be centered and function as one; in order to protect your mind and body, it is essential to first guide and lead others with your hands. You must understand thoroughly how to guide your opponent in one direction and down him in that same direction. When your opponent wants to pull, you must learn to anticipate and direct such a pull. When you achieve success in *bujutsu*[19] training you sense immediately what the opponent lacks and fulfill it; that is, you must perceive the openings in your opponent's position—that which is lacking—and apply a technique there. Perceiving an opponent's weakness in such a manner is *budō*. True *budō*, however, is not for the sole purpose of destroying an opponent; it is far better to defeat an opponent spiritually [by making him realize the folly of his actions] and then he will gladly abandon his attack. True *budō* is for the purpose of establishing harmony. Mind and body are the actualized forms of water and fire; unified in spirit, we must ceaselessly train in the techniques of harmonization. If the opponent grabs your wrist, step back with the left leg, guide him in that direction, hold his arm while striking his face, and down him.

All the *bujutsu* of Japan manifest the teachings of heaven and earth. For example, when one is surrounded by enemies attacking simultaneously with spears, one must look upon them as a single opponent and cut through the crowd with a steady mind.

The ancients used pillars and trees as shields, but that is a mistake. Nor should we rely on others for protection. Our spirit is the true shield. When facing numerous opponents, draw out their attacks, enter directly, and turn behind their thrusting spears; by applying this principle one can shatter the circle and escape to safe ground. When surrounded apply this same principle; enter and turn, taking care not to break your own posture, and stymie your opponents.

Learn the proper dimensions [of the truth], do not train in the ways of deceit, and do not violate the sacred trust that you have received from the gods: each person is a miniature universe.

The practice of *bujutsu* is to defeat an opponent in this fashion; one must train so that such principles permeate one's body. When surrounded by a host of enemies think of them as one; when facing a single foe think of him as many. This is the best strategy. Learn how to use the one to strike the ten thousand without offering your opponent the slightest opening. Build *yamato-damashii* like this, free of any slack in mind and body. Unify upper, middle, and lower; truly enter, turn, and blend with your opponents, front and back, left and right. It is essential to foster such presence of mind continuously in regular training.

In extreme situations, the entire world becomes our foe; at such critical times, this kind of unity of mind and technique is essential—do not let your heart waver!

The human body is a creation of the divine spirit. Just as a single beam of light can disperse the darkness, we should train and train intently to acquire such a quality.

In a secret training manual written by an ancient worthy, there is the following statement: "*Bujutsu* must be applied just like a sunbeam flooding a room with light as soon as the door opens a crack." More than that, the light of our practice must be able to penetrate screens, walls, rocks, or any other material. In our path, our souls, our bodies, and everything else belong to the divine. A warrior's purpose is to master, according to the august presence, martial techniques that vivify both the manifest and hidden worlds.

Repeatedly train in the manifest world, train in the realm of the hidden until you can freely dwell continuously in both spheres. That is the spirit we need in order to bring the hidden virtues of sincerity and fidelity out into the open and make them increasingly known throughout the world.

The Path is exceedingly vast, reflecting the grand design of the hidden and manifest realms. A warrior is a living shrine of the divine who must serve that grand purpose. Always imagine yourself on the battlefield under the fiercest attack; never forget this crucial element of training. Never lose your identity; purify yourself to create a pristine, blameless world.

6. REAR TECHNIQUE TRAINING

1. Through the practice of rear techniques, one learns how to prepare one's mind and body against attacks from all directions, beginning with attacks from behind, and how to handle opponents freely. When an opponent unexpectedly appears behind you, all your senses must be alert, allowing you to discern his movements—this is an important aspect of *bujutsu* practice. The key to rear techniques is immediately to sense the presence of another person behind you; as soon as the opponent attempts to grab you from the rear, you must open the eyes of your heart and the window of your mind, follow your intuition, and move swiftly and surely to the proper position to counter the attack. Attacks from the rear are extremely dangerous and difficult to deal with. If you are off guard and inattentive to an unseen enemy, you will be caught unaware. It is essential always to exercise care in this regard. Even though the opponent is in front initially, if he has a keen *bujutsu* sense, he will be able to get behind you despite your counter moves, and put you in a precarious position.

It is essential to train against grabs from the rear; one must train diligently to develop the enlightened ability to adapt and to turn freely to the left, right, front, or back in order to avoid and down opponents. Rear techniques are meant to foster one's sixth sense. In this kind of *bujutsu,* we learn to function intuitively. Every day we must drill ourselves in order to develop intuition and swift responses. If this is mastered, we can handle an opponent as soon as he attempts to grab from behind by proceeding to the front and throwing him.

2. Grabbing the collar from the rear works on the same principle as a straight cut delivered directly behind an opponent. Thus, as soon as the collar is grasped you must move swiftly and seize the initiative from the opponent by striking his face and/or solar plexus. This closes the window of his mind.

In actual combat, as soon as the opponent moves to attack from the rear, turn in a flash and take a stance that allows you to attack his right (left) side; or turn in around him and down him from the right. In rear techniques, hip stability is vital, and we must strengthen that part of the body through daily training.

In rear techniques in which your opponent grabs your hand as you strike his face, swiftly step inside behind his right side with your left foot, pull him down, and then throw him; or step to his left with your right foot, turn, and throw him.

The above explanations are a distillation of ten thousand techniques; all techniques are derived from the same deep principles. All of the details of strategy and technique cannot possibly be described in books. Put them into practice and obtain instruction first-hand.

ILLUSTRATION AND EXPLANATION OF SELECTED TECHNIQUES

1. PRECAUTIONS FOR TRAINING

1. The original intent of *bujutsu* was to kill an enemy with one blow; since all techniques can be lethal, observe the instructor's directions and do not engage in contests of strength.

2. *Bujutsu* is an art in which the one is used to strike the many. Therefore, train yourself always to be mindful of, and alert to, opponents in the four and the eight directions.

3. Always train in a vibrant and joyful manner.

4. The instructor can only impart a small portion of the teaching; only through ceaseless training can you obtain the necessary experience allowing you to bring these mysteries alive. Hence, do not chase after many techniques; one by one, make each technique your own.

5. In daily training, begin with basic movements to strengthen the body without overexertion. Spend the first ten minutes warming up, and there will be no fear of injury, even for old people. Enjoy yourself in training and strive to comprehend its true purpose.

6. Training in *bujutsu* is to foster *yamato-damashii* and to build one's character. The techniques are transmitted from person to person, on an individual basis, and should not be disclosed indiscriminately to the public.[20] Such secret techniques should not be misused for evil purposes.

2. BASIC MOVEMENTS

1. Stance

Fill yourself with *ki*, assume a *hanmi* [21] stance with your feet apart, opened at a sixty-degree angle, [22] and face your opponent with a flexible *aiki* posture (**1**).

The exact stance depends upon time, place, and terrain; further, it must arise in accordance with divine principles. A good stance reflects a proper frame of mind.

Both the front foot and the back foot should be open at a sixty-degree angle. The reason for this will become clear in practice.

Note: During practice be ever mindful of your opponent's stance and his relative distance; assume, accordingly, a left or right stance. When the movement ends, it is essential that your feet should always be open at a sixty-degree angle. If you face your opponent full of openings you will be at a great disadvantage.

1

2. Irimi

Uke: [23] Grasp your partner's left wrist with your right hand (**2**).

2

Tori:[24] Put strength into the fingertips of your left hand, turn the palm of your hand upward, slide forward diagonally, and enter deeply to your partner's right (3). At the same time remain aware of possible attacks from the rear. Grab your partner's right wrist from underneath with your right hand, release his grip, and strike his face (4). Slide in further, grab his collar (or pin his hips against your body),[25] step forward on your right foot bringing your partner's arm around his neck, and then down him (5, 6). During this last part of the technique, it is vital to put strength into the fingertips of your right hand and bring your arm down to the inside.

3   4

5   6

3. Tai-no-henka to the left and right

Uke: Same attack as in No. 2.

Tori: Concentrate your spirit in the fingertips of your left hand, pivot on your front foot, making a large half-turn, and position yourself to your opponent's right, remaining aware of possible attacks from the rear (7, 8). When executing body turns, keep your feet open at a sixty-degree angle—the most stable posture.

Uke: Uke should move slightly forward when *tori* completes his turn, thus facilitating *tori*'s movement.

Note: Always practice body turns from both the left and right sides.

7   8

4. *Irimi-tenkan*

Enter from the left foot and immediately execute a body turn. [Not illustrated.]

3. EMPTY HAND AGAINST EMPTY HAND

SHŌMEN

5.

Same stances as in No. 1.

Tori: Step out on your right foot and strike directly at your opponent's face with your right *te-gatana* and punch his ribs with your left fist (9). [The punch is not shown.][26]

Uke: Receive your opponent's attack with the right arm.

Tori: Put strength in your right arm and cut down sharply, holding your opponent's wrist and controlling his right elbow (10). Step in to his right with your left foot, keeping his right arm against your body, and pull him to your front (11). Move forward and pin him to the ground. (This is called Pin Number One.) You can then pin your partner's right arm with your legs and strike his neck with your right *te-gatana* (12).

Note: It is essential to advance forcefully (using both hands and both feet in coordination) and to pin your opponent's arm at a right angle.

9

10

11

12

6.

When your opponent strikes first with *shōmen*, turn around the attack with *irimi-tenkan*, use your right hand to receive the blow, and then control your opponent as described in No. 5. [Not illustrated.]

7.

Tori: Fill yourself with *ki* and invite your opponent to strike with *shōmen*.

Uke: Raise your right *te-gatana* high, step forward on your right foot, and deliver a *shōmen* strike.

Tori: Enter to your opponent's right, strike his ribs with your left fist, and use your right *te-gatana* to cut down his attack (**13**). Turn deeply behind your opponent and throw him (as outlined in No. 2) with the added element of a strong push to the chin (**14, 15, 16**).

Note: In actual combat, strike your opponent's face with full force.

13

14

15

16

8.

Tori: Fill yourself with *ki* and invite your opponent to strike with *shōmen.*

Uke: Deliver a *shōmen* strike with your right *te-gatana* (**17**).

Tori: Advance on the left foot and execute *irimi-tenkan* (or, as the case may be, *tai-no-henka*) as you use your left *te-gatana* to strike down on your opponent's right wrist (**18**). Grab his right hand on the outside, pressing your thumb against the base of his ring and little fingers, step back on your left foot while powerfully twisting his fist with both of your hands, and down him (19). Apply the hold illustrated in (20). This will immobilize your opponent's hands and feet.

17

18

19

20

9.

Tori: Attack your opponent's face and ribs as described in No. 5.

Uke: Receive the attack with your right hand.

Tori: Make a big turn and use your right hand to cut down and direct your opponent's wrist. Slide in and get a reverse grip on his wrist, bring it against your chest, and grasp his forearm with your left hand. Twist forcefully and control him, as shown (21, 22, 23). Step back, pull him to the ground, and pin his right arm with both hands (24). This is called "Pin Number Two."

21   22

23   24

10.

Tori: Same as in No. 9.

Uke: Same as in No. 9.

Tori: After making a big turn (**25**), grab your opponent's right fingers, and twist to the right with a slight turn up and back. Apply a reverse twist with your left hand while striking his face with your right fist (**26**). Pull back on your left foot, control his right elbow with a reverse grip using your right hand, and pull him down to the right (**27**). (This is called Pin Number Three.) Then sit next to your opponent's right and pin him, forming a cross with your hands (**28**).

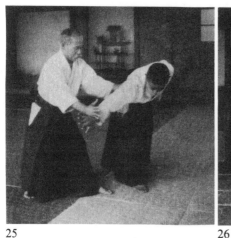

25   26

27   28

YOKOMEN

11.

Tori: Fill yourself with *ki* and invite your opponent to deliver a *yokomen* strike.

Uke: Step forward on your right foot and deliver a *yokomen* strike with your right *te-gatana* to the left side of your opponent's head.

Tori: Advance slightly on your left foot and with your left *te-gatana* neutralize your opponent's attack, while simultaneously striking his face with your right hand (**29**). Then enter deeply to his side, and cut down his attacking *te-gatana* with your own right *te-gatana*, while striking his ribs with your left fist (**30**). Next use your right arm to down him (**31**).

29   30

31

12.

Training in *yokomen* attacks contains the essence of all techniques.

Tori: Fill yourself with *ki* and invite your opponent to deliver a *yokomen* strike.

Uke: Deliver a *yokomen* blow as in No. 11.

Tori: Open slightly to the left and neutralize your opponent's attack with your left *te-gatana* while simultaneously striking his face with your right hand. Grasp his right wrist with your left hand, then with both hands, and raise his arm above your head as you step forward with the left foot (**32, 33**). Next turn 180 degrees and throw him [as if cutting through an opponent attacking from the rear (**34**)].

Note: It is necessary to think of your opponent's right arm as a striking sword. Also, your right thumb should be on his pulse.

32   33   34

13.

Tori: Your opponent attacks with a *yokomen* strike (as in No. 11). Enter to his rear, grasp his wrist from underneath with your right hand, step back, and bring him down with Pin Number One (35, 36).[27]

35   36

14.

Tori: In this case apply the movements described in No. 10 and use Pin Number Two [or Three] (37).

15.

Tori: As described in No. 11, execute *irimi-tenkan,* using your right *te-gatana* to control your opponent's attack, cut down low, and then hold his right arm with both hands (38). Step forward and cut down, as with a sword, and pin your opponent (39, 40).

48

Note: Placement of your left hand in this technique is as follows: hold your opponent's wrist tightly with both the little and ring fingers and use the knuckle at the base of the index finger to apply strong pressure to his pulse. (This is known as "Pin Number Four.")

37

38   39   40

TRAINING IN THROWS

16.

Uke: Take a half step forward on your right foot and grab your opponent's hands.

Tori: Turn out to the right, take a half step forward on your right foot, and then a big step in with your left foot. Use your right hand to hold your opponent's wrist. (Put strength into the fingers of your left hand and raise his hand with your shoulder; hold his arm tightly with your right hand, keeping your thumb on his pulse, and pull him toward you (**41**).) Bring his arm up over your head (**42, 43**), turn approximately 180 degrees, pivoting on the left foot (**44**), and throw him to the back (as if cutting through an attacker from the rear (**45**).) After the throw is completed, pin your opponent's right arm with your right hand, reversing him (**46**).

41

42

43

44

45

46

17.

Uke: Same as above.

Tori: Pivot on your left foot, sweep to the right, and throw as described in the previous technique. [Not illustrated.]

TRAINING IN AIKI

Through the virtue of training, understanding of *aiki* is acquired naturally. Precise instructions must be imparted orally.

18.

When your opponent grabs your wrist (**47, 48**).

47   48

19.

When your opponent grabs both hands (**49, 50, 51**).

49   50   51

20.

When your opponent thrusts (**52, 53, 54**).

52   53   54

21. Training in yokomen

Uke: Deliver a *yokomen* strike with your right hand.

Tori: Step forward on your left foot, and use your left *te-gatana* to neutralize your opponent's attack, simultaneously striking his face [and down him] (**55**).

55

TRAINING IN REAR TECHNIQUES

22.

Uke: Grab hold of your opponent's collar and pull (**56**).

Tori: As soon as your opponent pulls, step out on the right foot, turn inside to his right with the left foot, and strike his face with your left *te-gatana* and his solar plexus with your right hand (**57**).

56   57

23.

Uke: Same attack as above.

Tori: Pull out on your right foot and strike your opponent's face with your *te-gatana* (leaving your right hand free to deal with other attackers (**58**).)

58

Uke: Block your opponent's blow with your left hand.

Tori: Take a big step back on your left foot, bring your opponent down to the front, control his arm with your right hand, attack his side with your left hand, and push him down (**59**).

59

24.

Uke: Grab hold of your opponent's collar from behind and push to the front (**60**).

Tori: As soon as your opponent pushes, take a step forward on your right foot, pivot to the left, strike his face with your left *te-gatana*, and throw him (**61**).

60   61

25.

Uke: Same as above.

Tori: When your opponent grabs your collar, pivot on your right foot to the outside, and use your right *te-gatana* to strike down on his arm (**62**). Then step behind your opponent on your right foot, strike his face with your right hand, and down him (**63**).

54

62   63

26.

Uke: Grab both of your opponent's wrists from behind (**64**).

Tori: Pull out on the left foot and raise both hands (**65**). Next step back on the right foot, simultaneously cutting down with both hands, and throw him to the front (**66**).

64   65   66

4. Empty Hand Against Sword

SHŌMEN

27.

Tori: Fill yourself with *ki* and invite your opponent to attack (**67**).

Uke: Deliver a *shōmen* cut.

Tori: As soon as your opponent cuts, move with the speed of the gods and enter deeply to his right with *irimi-tenkan*. Strike your opponent's right wrist with your left *te-gatana*, remaining aware of possible attackers to the rear, and strike his face with your right fist (**68**). Apply the technique described in No. 8 [i.e., *kote-gaeshi*], and down your opponent (**69, 70**). (In this case, it is necessary to control his hand and sword with the little and ring fingers of your right hand.) Next turn your opponent around to the left, pin him face down, take the sword, and hold it to his neck (**71**).

67   68

69   70   71

28.

Tori: Same as above.

Uke: Deliver a *shōmen* cut.

Tori: Enter and strike your opponent's ribs and face (**72**). Next apply the technique described in No. 7 [i.e., *irimi-nage*] and down him (**73, 74**).

72

73

74

29.

Tori: With your right foot forward, assume a *ki*-filled stance and invite your opponent to strike (75).

Uke: Deliver a *shōmen* cut.

Tori: Enter to your opponent's left side and strike his solar plexus with your right fist (76). Then grab the handle of his sword with your left hand and strike his face with your right *te-gatana* (77).

30.

In order to sense the direction of the sword's *ki,* it is necessary to develop keen perception.

Tori: Fill yourself with *ki* and invite your opponent to strike.

Uke: Deliver a *shōmen* cut from *jōdan.*[28]

Tori: As soon as your opponent attacks, turn either to the left or right as the occasion demands. You must practice until you can move naturally and smoothly, even under the direct attack of a sword. [Not illustrated.]

Explanation: As soon as an enemy cuts, an opening appears in his defense; during the training described here, you will learn to fill yourself with *ki*, perceive that weakness, and clearly discern the path of the blade as you track it in your mind. Iron is full of impurities that weaken it; through forging it becomes steel and is transformed into a razor-sharp sword. A peerless Masamune blade[29] is the result of ceaseless forging; human beings also develop in a similar manner. Mutually train until all weakness vanishes; then, when there is a cut or a thrust, your technique will be perfect. Foster such *ki* in order to create a sincere human being.

75

76

77

YOKOMEN AND CHEST ATTACKS

31.

To be imparted by oral instruction.

KNIFE ATTACKS

32.

Against a knife thrust (or a pistol attack), apply technique No. 7 [i.e., *irimi-nage*] (78).

78

33.

Apply technique No. 8 [i.e., *kote-gaeshi*] (79).

79

34.

Uke: Deliver a *shōmen* attack with a knife.

Tori: When your opponent attacks, enter, grab his right forearm with your right hand, and apply Pin Number One (**80, 81**).[30]

80   81

5. SWORD AGAINST SWORD

WRIST CUTS

35.

Tori: Fill yourself with *ki* and invite your opponent to strike your wrist (**82**).

Uke: Deliver a strike to your opponent's wrist.

Tori: Open widely to the left and cut your opponent's wrist (**83**).

82   83

ATTACKS TO THE HEAD

36.

Tori: Fill yourself with *ki* and lead your opponent's right hand.

Uke: Deliver a *shōmen* cut (84).

Tori: Execute *irimi-tenkan* to the right and strike his head (85).

84

85

37.

Tori: Fill yourself with *ki* and invite your opponent to strike.

Uke: Deliver a *shōmen* cut.

Tori: Enter and strike his head. [Not illustrated.]

Note: The principle of striking the opponent without being struck oneself is to be imparted by oral instruction.

38.

Tori: Same as above (**86**).

Uke: Deliver a *shōmen* cut.

Tori: Enter, turn the blade up, and thrust at your opponent's chest (**87**). Then strike his head (**88**) and thrust again (**89**).

86   87

88   89

6. BAYONET ATTACKS

39.

Tori: Assume a right *aiki* stance and invite your opponent to attack (**90**).

Uke: Make a straight thrust.

Tori: Enter and cut down on your opponent's left forearm with your right *te-gatana* (**91**). Then grasp his collar from behind and strike his face with your left *te-gatana* (**92**).

90   91   92

40.

Uke: Same as above.

Tori: As in the previous technique, draw out your opponent's attack, but this time, grab the bayonet with both hands, step forward on your right foot, and throw him (**93, 94**).

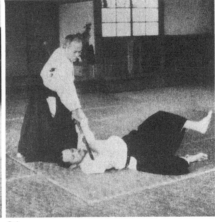

93   94

41.

Uke: Same as above.

Tori: Enter as in No. 39, but this time grab the bayonet with your left hand from underneath, pull back on your left foot, and apply a reverse lock to your opponent's left elbow with your right forearm (**95, 96**).

95   96

42.

Tori: Assume a left *aiki* stance and face your opponent (**97**).

Uke: Same as above.

Tori: Enter and strike your opponent's face with your left *te-gatana* and his forearm with your right (**98**). Grasp the bayonet with both hands, step in with the right foot, and down him (**99**).

97   98   99

43. Bayonet against bayonet

Tori: Fill yourself with *ki* and invite the opponent to attack.

Uke: Same as above.

Tori: As soon as the opponent thrusts, enter to the left with *irimi-tenkan* and pierce him (**100**).

100

Note: Against a spear attack, the movements are basically the same as those used against the bayonet (**101, 102, 103, 104**).

101

102

103

104

7. CONCLUDING EXERCISES

TAI-NO-HENKA

44. Application of training in throws

Uke: Grab hold of your partner's wrists.

Tori: As in practicing a throw, put strength into your fingertips, step forward with your left foot, lift both hands above your head, pivot on your left foot, and cut down, keeping your partner suspended on your hips (**105**). Next reverse your position, turn to your partner's right side, and apply the same technique (**106**). Repeat this exercise to the rear.

105   106

DEVELOPING KI POWER

45.

Face your partner in *seiza* (**107**).

Uke: Grab your opponent's wrists.

Tori: Turn your palms inward, put strength into your fingertips, concentrate your spirit, raise your hands like a sword, and push your opponent back with both forearms (**108, 109**). Proceed forward on the right knee, rise up, and throw your opponent to the left (**110, 111**).

Note: When you throw, open both hands slightly, direct your right hand toward your opponent's left shoulder, and push down to your left. If you pull your hands toward your own body, the technique will not be effective.

107

108

109

110

111

46.

Uke: Same as above.

Tori: As in No. 45. This time turn both palms outward, extend your arms to the left, and throw your opponent (**112, 113**).

112

113

47.

Uke: Same as above.

Tori: Raise your right hand in the direction of your opponent's left shoulder, extend your left hand under his arm, and push him down to the left (**114, 115**).

114

115

48.

Uke: Same as above.

Tori: Move both hands in a scooping motion and throw your opponent to the right [or left] (**116, 117**).

116

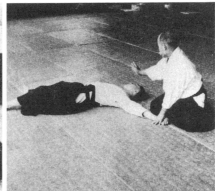
117

DEVELOPING ARM POWER

49.

To be imparted by oral instruction.

BACK STRETCH

50.

Tori: Grab hold of your partner's wrists (**118**).

Uke: Turn your right foot out to the left, step in, and stretch your partner across your back (**119**).[31]

Tori: After being stretched, release your grip, and slide down to the ground.

118

119

THE SECRETS OF BUDŌ

(SPIRITUAL POEMS)

Sincerity!
Cultivate this virtue
and realize
the profound truth that
the manifest and hidden are one.

Master the divine
techniques of *aiki*
and no enemy
will dare to
challenge you.

Seeing me before him
the enemy attacks
but by that time
I am already
standing behind him.

I let the deluded enemy
attack my form
but instantly
I stand behind him
and cut down the foe.

Left and right
avoid all
cuts and parries;
seize your opponents' minds
and scatter them all.

Surrounded by a forest
of enemy spears—
enter deeply and
learn to use your mind
as a shield.

A host of enemies
rush into attack—
think of them as
a single foe
and deal with them accordingly.

> Even when called out
> by a single foe,
> remain on guard,
> for you are always surrounded
> by a host of enemies.

Translator's Notes

1. *budō*: the Path of Martial Valor, the Way of a Warrior. This is a way of life dedicated to peace and enlightened action. Here *budō* is used in both the general sense of Japanese martial traditions and the more specific manifestion of Morihei's *aiki-budō*, which eventually led to the formulation of aikidō. Sometimes in the text the abbreviation *bu* is used, but for ease of comprehension, the more formal term *budō* is used throughout the translation.

2. In Morihei's system, the cosmos is activated and sustained through the interaction of water (*mizu*) and fire (*ka*). Water is matter; fire is spirit. In combination, they form *iki*, life, breath, and *kami*, the divine.

3. *kotodama*: the esoteric science of "sound-spirit." *Kotodama* are the pure sounds that crystallize as vibrations of various concentrations which are then perceived as sound, color, and form. Every principle and technique has a *kotodama*, a sacred vibration that contains its essence; if one understands the significance of the *kotodama*, one can grasp its function (i.e., water) and merge with its spirit (i.e., fire).

4. *ki*: the subtle energy that fills and propels the universe; the life force that holds creation together.

5. *dōka*: didactic poems composed, in the 5-7-5-7-7 syllable mode, by masters to inspire and instruct their disciples.

6. This *dōka* describes *kiai*, shouts of perfectly controlled, concentrated energy that can shatter an opponent's defenses.

7. This is the double-edged sword (*tsurugi*) of wisdom and purification, the spiritual sword of one's mind to be applied to every technique, either literally or symbolically.

8. *kannagara*: this term occurs frequently in the text. It refers to a state in which one is perfectly attuned to the functioning of the divine in all aspects of life. In such an ideal state, one acts naturally, spontaneously, and sincerely, free of artifice and duplicity. "Divine" refers not to something supernatural, but to anything that inspires reverence and manifests goodness, purity, and beauty.

9. *aiki*: spiritual harmonization, the coming together of all elements in perfect unity.

10. *Izu-no-me-no-kami*: a Shintō deity that cleans the world of filth and corruption.

11. *makoto*: oneness in word and deed; truly following the order of the universe.

12. *yamato-damashii*: the spirit of ancient Japan. Nowadays best interpreted as the manifestation of all that is good and true in human nature.

13. *irimi*: on the physical level, this means to enter to the side in order to avoid an opponent's attack; on the spiritual level, it means to penetrate and defuse an aggressive force.

14. *kokyū*: *prana*, the vital breath of life, the universal current of vibrant energy. Technically, *kokyū* refers to proper timing and a steady, unimpeded flow of power.

15. *tai-no-henka*: body-turn, pivoting on one foot, and usually involving a sweep of 180 degrees.

16. *irimi-tenkan*: enter and turn, a combination of *irimi* and *tai-no-henka* applied according to circumstances. In the original text the term *irimi-tenka*, "turn and transform," was used, but to facilitate understanding, the modern name of the technique has been used throughout the translation.

17. *shōmen*: a strike delivered directly to the crown of your opponent's head.

18. This refers to a famous incident in Shintō mythology. The absence of the Sun Goddess, who was sulking in a cave covered with a stone door, was depriving the earth of light and heat. She was enticed out of the cave by the collective effort of the gods, who persuaded her to open the stone door. In this modern era, Morihei is suggesting that all human beings should bind together so that our polluted world of death and destruction will be bathed once more in the light of truth and beauty.

19. *bujutsu*: martial art, the application and execution of martial techniques.

20. The text literally says: ". . . create sincere Japanese people . . . and do not show these techniques to others."

21. *hanmi*: a "half-body" stance. i.e., facing your opponent at an angle with one foot forward.

22. Initially, the angle formed by the feet seems closer to ninety degrees, but during the execution of the techniques, both feet point out at a sixty degree angle. e.g., in illustrations 21, 32, 33, and 34.

23. *uke*: the one who is on the receiving end of the technique.

24. *tori*: the one who executes the technique. In the original text the word *shi* was used.

25. As in *sokumen irimi-nage*. (See page 84.)

26. For an illustration of the punch, see page 101.

27. In the original text 35, 36, and 37 were in the wrong order. The technique described here is called Pin Number Five in modern aikidō.

28. *jōdan*: a stance with the sword held above one's head.

29. Swords made by the medieval swordsmith Masamune are considered to be the finest ever forged in Japan.

30. This is now known as Pin Number Five. (See note 25.)

31. In this case, Morihei acts as *uke*.

PART III

NOMA DŌJŌ
TECHNIQUES

Noma Dōjō Techniques

The Noma Dōjō Techniques were photographed in the private dōjō of Seiji Noma, then president of Kodansha, Ltd., in 1936, when Morihei was fifty-three years old. Shigemi Yonekawa served as uke, and the techniques were shot in several sessions. Morihei took his own injunction to train in a "vibrant and joyful manner" to heart—he can be seen smiling in several of the photographs.

The photographs were preserved in five scrapbooks, but were removed in random order when rephotographed recently (the original negatives having long since vanished). Consequently, all of the photographs had to be rearranged for publication.

Since there were no technical descriptions or directions attached to the original photographs, those published here have been grouped according to technique, and described by modern aikidō terminology to facilitate comprehension.

When studying the photographs, it is important to note that they were taken with comparatively primitive "stop-action" photography. Morihei posed at each stage of the technique, and then the camera was usually moved to a different position to refocus, or to capture a subsequent movement from another angle, resulting in a somewhat different perspective for each shot. It also appears that there were several takes for some of the techniques that were then combined into a sequence. In certain cases there are missing segments that must be supplied by visualization. In short the photographs, in many cases, are not truly sequential.

For the sake of comparison, several sequences of photographs taken in Wakayama in 1951, when Morihei was sixty-eight years old, are included throughout this section. The differences between Morihei's execution of the technique in the pre- and postwar periods is often contrasted, but as we can see by comparing the Noma Dōjō Techniques (1936) and Wakayama (1951), the essence of Morihei's art remained the same.

The photographs in this section afford students the precious opportunity to further observe how Morihei himself actually practiced the techniques of aiki, techniques that can assist us in attaining harmony with nature and link us to the highest principles of life.

John Stevens

Shihō-nage
hanmi-hantachi

1

2

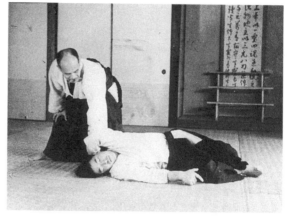

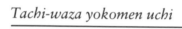

Tachi-waza yokomen uchi

Irimi-nage

Suwari waza (Wakayama)

Suwari-waza

Kata-dori chokusen no irimi

Yokomen-uchi irimi-nage

Sokumen Irimi-nage
Suwari-waza

1

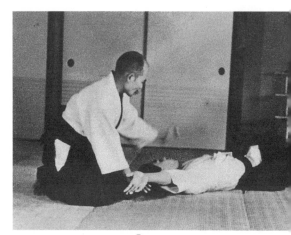

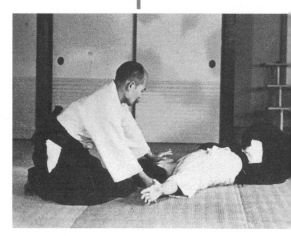

2

3

4

Kote-gaeshi
Suwari-waza

Sumi-otoshi
Suwari-waza

1

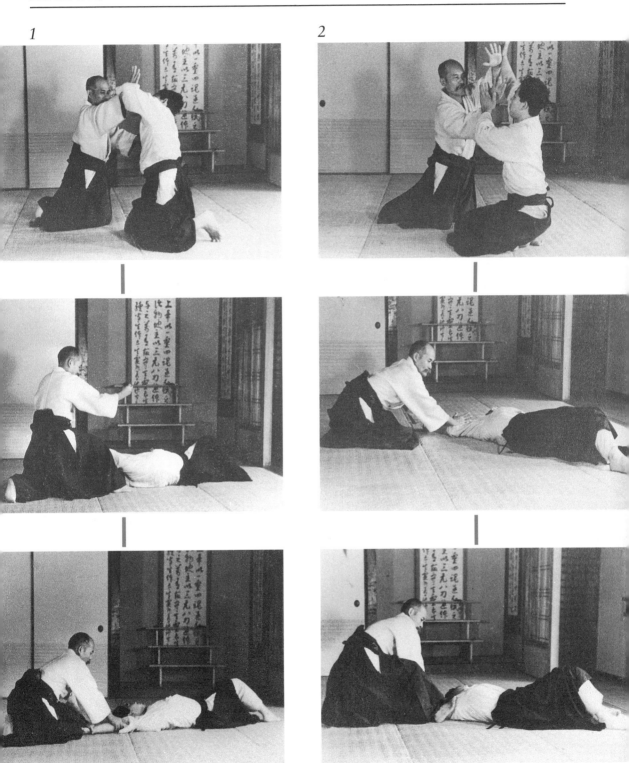

2

5

6

Tenchi-nage

1

2

Kokyū-nage

1 Suwari-waza

2 Tachi-waza
(the initial standing stance is not shown)

91

5 (to the front)

6 (to the rear)

(Wakayama)

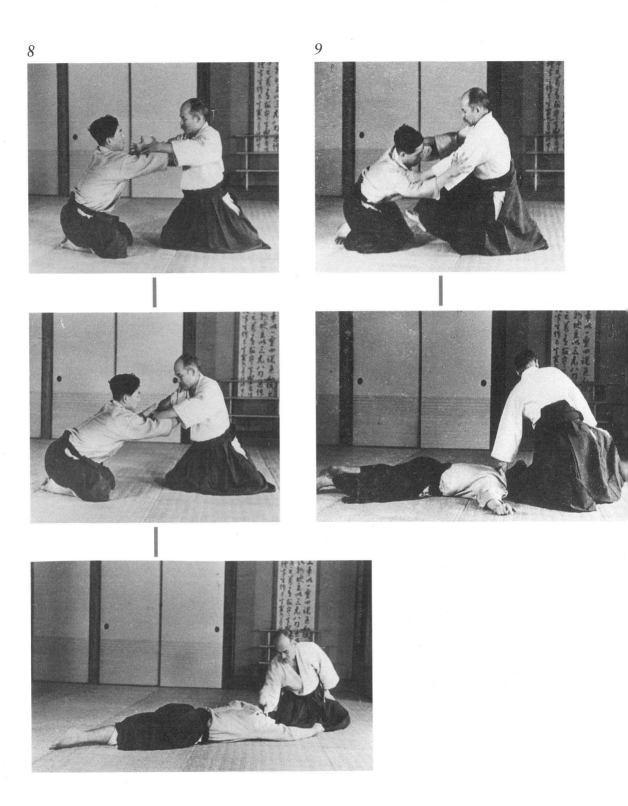

10

11

(reverse grip)

12

13

1

2 *(sode-dori)*

(ryōte-dori)

Shōmen- (or Yokomen-) uchi kokyū-nage

1 (suwari)

2 (tachi)

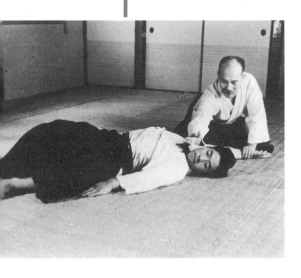

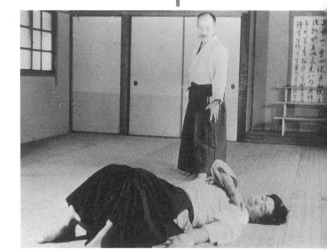

1

2

Ikkyō osae
Tachi-waza basic technique

Kata-dori ikkyō   (Wakayama)

(Ikkyō-nage)

1

Pin Variation

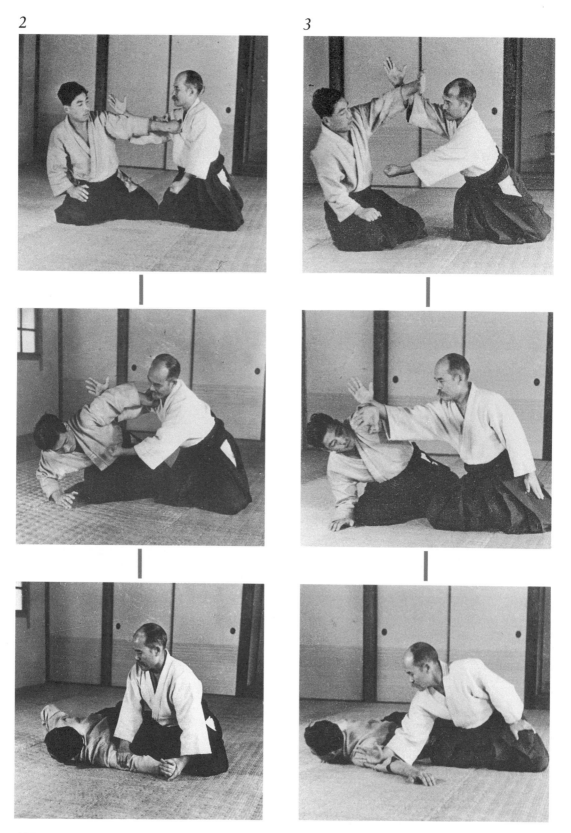

1

2

Variation (entry to the side)

1

2

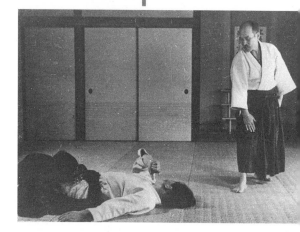

Ude-osae
Suwari-waza

1

(reverse grip)

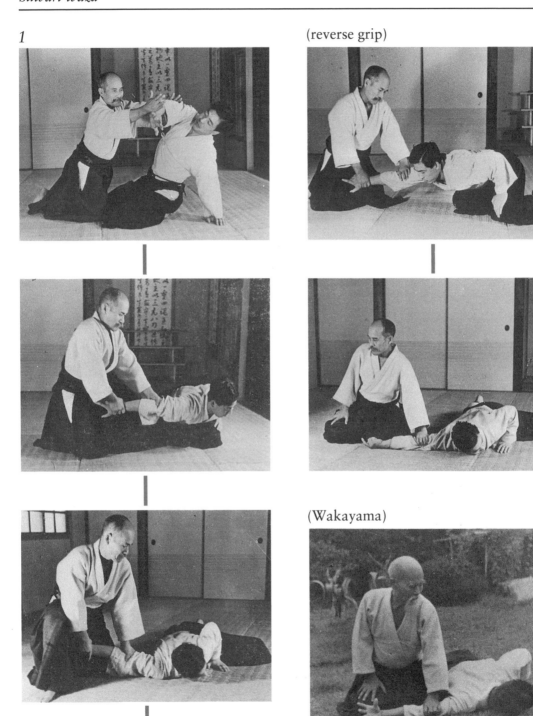

(Wakayama)

2

3

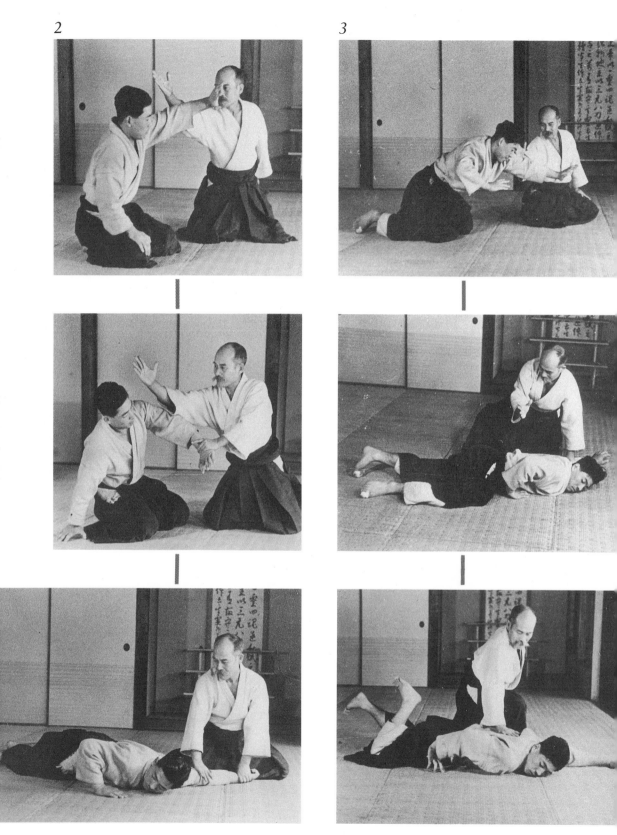

4

Pin Variations

1

2

3

1

2

Nikkyō osae
Suwari-waza

Basic Technique

(seen from the front)

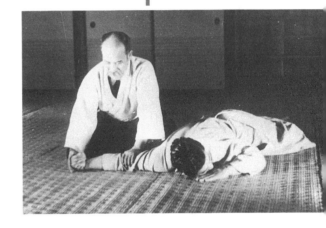

(the nikkyō grip)

(Wakayama)

1   **2**

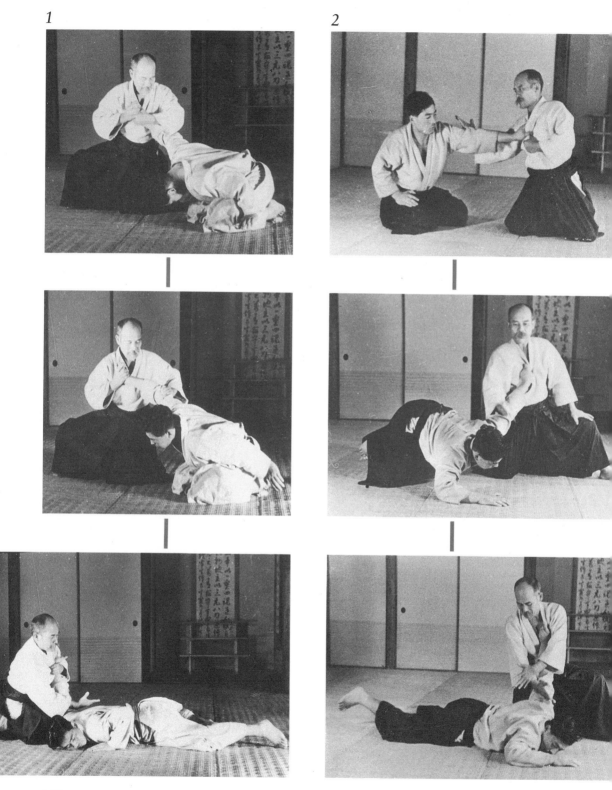

1

2

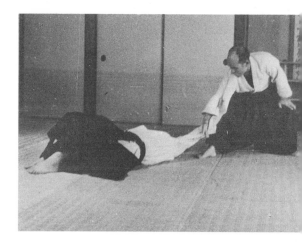

Hiji-jime osae
Suwari-waza

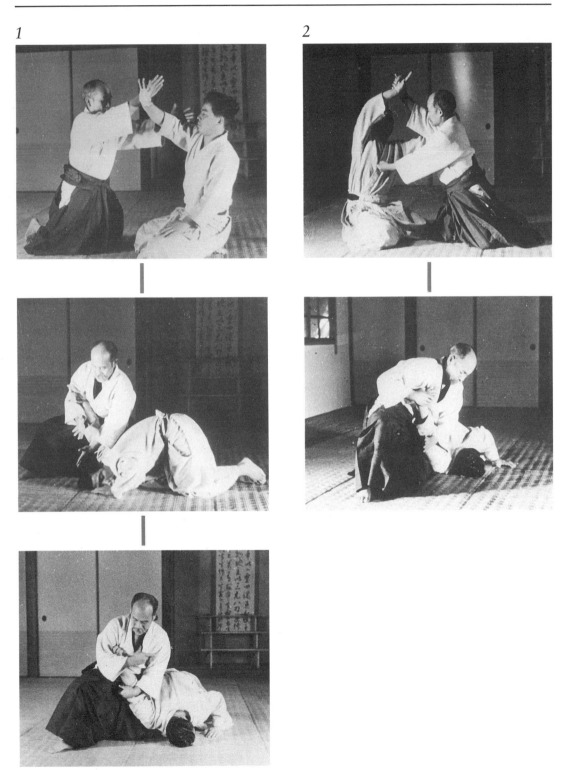

1

2

Juji-nage
Suwari-waza

1

2 (Wakayama)

Kubi-nage
Suwari-waza

1

2 (Wakayama)

Koshi-nage
suwari-waza

1

2

1   2

(ganseki-otoshi)

1

(side view)

2

3

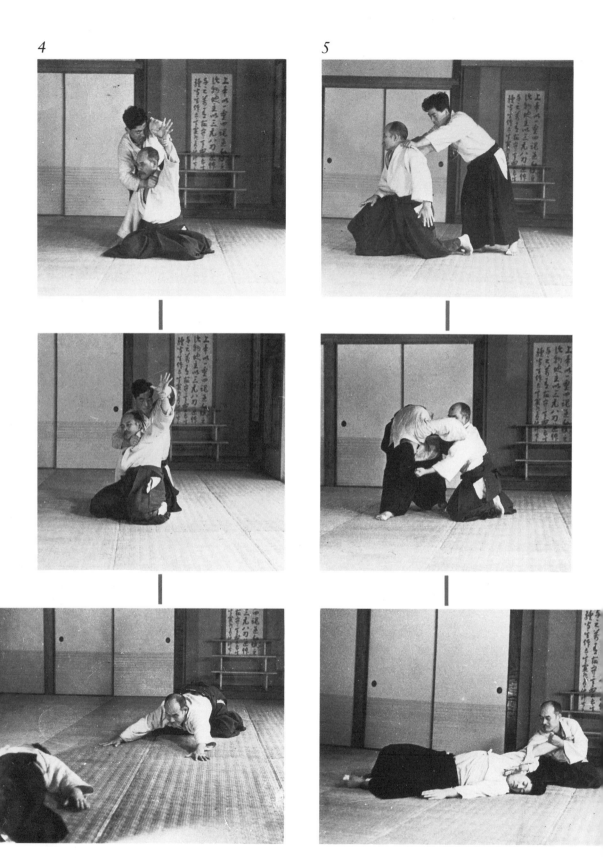